Exploring the Underworld: Deviant Behavior in Sociological Studies for Students

Ivaan Mier

Copyright © [2023]

Title: Exploring the Underworld: Deviant Behavior in Sociological Studies for Students
Author's: Ivaan Mier

This book was printed and published by [Publisher's: **Ivaan Mier**] in [2023]

ISBN:

TABLE OF CONTENT

Chapter 3: Types of Deviant Behavior 20

Chapter 7: Deviant Behavior and Technology 67

Chapter 8: Consequences of Deviant Behavior 73

Chapter 9: Researching Deviant Behavior 80

Chapter 1: Introduction to Deviant Behavior Sociology

Defining Deviant Behavior

Deviant behavior is a complex and multifaceted concept that has fascinated sociologists for decades. In order to fully understand and analyze deviant behavior, it is essential to first establish a clear definition of what constitutes deviance within a sociological context.

Deviance refers to any behavior that violates societal norms and expectations. These norms are the unwritten rules that guide our behavior and dictate what is considered acceptable and unacceptable in a particular society or culture. Deviant behavior, therefore, encompasses actions, attitudes, and beliefs that diverge from these established norms.

However, it is important to note that deviance is not an absolute concept. What may be considered deviant in one society or time period may be completely acceptable in another. Deviance is not inherently negative or positive; it is simply a departure from the norm. Sociologists recognize that deviant behavior can vary across different social groups, geographical locations, and historical periods.

Deviant behavior can manifest in a variety of forms. It can range from relatively harmless acts, such as wearing unconventional clothing or engaging in unconventional hobbies, to more serious transgressions, such as criminal activities or engaging in harmful behaviors. It is crucial to remember that deviance is a socially constructed concept influenced by societal power dynamics and cultural values.

Sociologists study deviant behavior to gain insights into the functioning of societies and the social forces that shape individual behavior. By analyzing deviance, sociologists can identify patterns, understand social control mechanisms, and assess the impact of deviant behavior on individuals and communities.

Furthermore, deviance is not limited to individuals. Societies, institutions, and groups can also exhibit deviant behavior. For instance, corporate fraud, political corruption, and hate crimes committed by organized groups are all examples of collective deviant behavior.

In conclusion, the subchapter "Defining Deviant Behavior" provides an introduction to the complex and ever-evolving concept of deviance within a sociological framework. By exploring the definition and understanding of deviant behavior, students of sociology can develop a deeper appreciation for the social forces that shape our lives and gain valuable insights into the dynamics of societies. Through studying deviant behavior, students can further their understanding of social norms, cultural values, and the impact of deviance on individuals and communities.

Understanding Social Norms

Social norms are a fundamental aspect of human societies. They are the unwritten rules that govern our behavior and shape our interactions with others. In the book "Exploring the Underworld: Deviant Behavior in Sociological Studies for Students," we delve into the intricate world of social norms and explore their significance in the field of sociology.

To comprehend social norms, we must first understand what they are. Social norms are the expectations and standards of behavior that are considered acceptable within a particular society or group. They guide our actions, beliefs, and values, defining what is deemed appropriate or inappropriate, moral or immoral, and normal or deviant.

In this subchapter, we will explore the origins and functions of social norms. We will delve into the mechanisms through which norms are established, reinforced, and challenged. From a sociological perspective, we will analyze how social norms shape our identities and influence our daily lives.

One key aspect of understanding social norms is recognizing their cultural relativity. What is considered normal in one society may be considered deviant in another. This highlights the dynamic nature of social norms and the influence of cultural, historical, and geographical factors in their formation.

Moreover, we will examine the different types of social norms, such as folkways, mores, and taboos. We will discuss how these norms are enforced through various social control mechanisms, such as formal laws, informal sanctions, and socialization processes.

Additionally, we will explore the consequences of deviating from social norms. Deviant behavior can lead to social stigma, ostracism, and even legal repercussions. By studying deviance, we gain insight into the boundaries of what is considered acceptable in society and how these boundaries are socially constructed.

Understanding social norms is essential for sociological studies as they provide a framework for analyzing human behavior, social interactions, and social structures. By examining deviant behavior and the societal responses to it, we gain a deeper understanding of the complexities of human societies.

This subchapter aims to equip students of sociology with a comprehensive understanding of social norms and their significance. It provides a solid foundation for further exploration into the fascinating realm of deviant behavior and its implications for society at large. Through engaging examples, case studies, and theoretical frameworks, students will develop a critical lens to analyze and interpret the intricacies of social norms in their own lives and the broader world around them.

Theoretical Perspectives on Deviant Behavior

In the realm of sociology, deviant behavior has always been a subject of great interest and debate. Understanding the reasons behind deviant behavior is crucial in order to comprehend the complexities of society and its norms. This subchapter explores various theoretical perspectives that sociologists have developed to explain deviant behavior, shedding light on the underlying causes and consequences of such actions.

One prominent theoretical perspective is the functionalist perspective, which suggests that deviant behavior serves a purpose within society. According to functionalists, deviance can act as a catalyst for social change by challenging existing norms and values. By examining deviance, sociologists can identify flaws in society and work towards rectifying them.

On the other hand, conflict theorists argue that deviant behavior is a result of power struggles within society. They believe that those with power and privilege define what is considered deviant, often to maintain their own dominance. Conflict theorists also emphasize that deviance is not evenly distributed among social groups, highlighting the unequal power dynamics that exist within society.

Symbolic interactionism, another theoretical perspective, focuses on how individuals construct meaning through social interaction. According to this perspective, deviant behavior is a response to the labels and stigmatization imposed by society. Individuals may adopt deviant roles or engage in deviant acts as a means of gaining social recognition or challenging societal expectations.

The social control theory suggests that deviant behavior occurs when an individual's bonds to society weaken. This theory posits that strong social bonds, such as family, school, and community, act as deterrents to deviance. When these bonds are weakened or absent, individuals are more likely to engage in deviant behavior.

Lastly, the feminist perspective examines deviant behavior through the lens of gender inequality. Feminist sociologists argue that traditional theories fail to consider the unique experiences and motivations of women in deviant acts. They highlight how gender roles and societal expectations contribute to the differential treatment of men and women in deviance.

By exploring these theoretical perspectives, students of sociology can gain a comprehensive understanding of deviant behavior and its societal implications. These perspectives provide a framework for analyzing the causes, consequences, and social responses to deviance. Ultimately, understanding deviant behavior is essential for creating more inclusive and equitable societies.

Chapter 2: Historical Context of Deviant Behavior

Early Sociological Studies on Deviance

Deviance, as a concept, has intrigued sociologists for centuries. Understanding why individuals engage in deviant behavior and how society reacts to such behavior has been a focal point in the field of sociology. In this subchapter, we will delve into the early sociological studies on deviance, exploring the foundations laid by influential scholars in the field.

One of the pioneering figures in the study of deviance was Emile Durkheim. His groundbreaking work, "The Rules of Sociological Method," published in 1895, established deviance as a social construct. Durkheim argued that deviance is not an inherent characteristic of individuals but rather a product of social norms and values. He emphasized the importance of social cohesion and integration in determining the occurrence of deviant behavior within a society. Durkheim's perspective paved the way for further research on the social causes and consequences of deviance.

Another influential sociologist, Robert Merton, expanded on Durkheim's ideas with his theory of structural strain. In his renowned work "Social Structure and Anomie," published in 1938, Merton examined the relationship between societal goals and the means individuals use to achieve them. According to Merton, when individuals are unable to attain their goals through legitimate means, they may resort to deviant behavior. This theory shed light on the role of social structure in shaping deviance and offered a framework for understanding the different forms of deviant behavior in society.

Howard Becker, in his seminal work "Outsiders: Studies in the Sociology of Deviance," published in 1963, challenged the traditional notion of deviance as a personal failing. Becker argued that deviance is a social construct influenced by the reactions of others. He introduced the concept of labeling theory, which posits that individuals become deviant when labeled as such by society. This theory shifted the focus from the deviant act itself to the social processes that label individuals as deviant, highlighting the role of power dynamics and social control.

These early sociological studies on deviance laid the groundwork for further research and theories in the field. They demonstrated the importance of considering the broader social context in understanding deviant behavior and challenged simplistic explanations that attribute deviance solely to individual characteristics. By examining the social causes, consequences, and reactions to deviance, sociologists have contributed significantly to our understanding of human behavior and the dynamics of society.

In conclusion, the early sociological studies on deviance have shaped the field of sociology and provided valuable insights into the social nature of deviant behavior. From Durkheim's emphasis on social integration to Merton's theory of structural strain and Becker's labeling theory, these scholars paved the way for further exploration of deviance within society. By studying these foundational works, students of sociology can gain a deeper understanding of the complexities surrounding deviant behavior and its impact on individuals and society as a whole.

Influence of Durkheim's Theory of Anomie

The Influence of Durkheim's Theory of Anomie

Émile Durkheim, a renowned sociologist of the late 19th and early 20th centuries, introduced the concept of anomie, which has had a significant impact on the field of sociology. Anomie refers to a state of normlessness or a breakdown of social norms, resulting in individuals feeling disconnected and alienated from society. In his groundbreaking work, "Suicide: A Study in Sociology," Durkheim explored the relationship between social integration and suicide rates, providing valuable insights into the influence of anomie on deviant behavior.

Durkheim argued that when individuals experience a lack of social integration, they are more prone to feelings of anomie, which can lead to deviant behavior. This is particularly relevant in modern societies characterized by rapid social changes, weakened social ties, and a diminished sense of community. Durkheim's theory of anomie sheds light on the link between societal factors and deviance, offering a sociological lens to understand the root causes of various forms of deviant behavior.

One area where Durkheim's theory of anomie has been particularly influential is the study of crime and delinquency. According to his perspective, crime is not solely the result of individual pathology, but rather a manifestation of societal dysfunction. Durkheim argued that when social norms are weak or inconsistent, individuals may resort to deviant behavior as a means of achieving their goals or satisfying their needs. His theory emphasizes the importance of social integration and the role of social institutions in preventing crime and promoting social cohesion.

Moreover, Durkheim's theory of anomie has also shaped our understanding of other forms of deviant behavior, such as substance abuse and mental health issues. The breakdown of social norms and lack of social integration can contribute to individuals seeking solace or escape through drug use or developing mental health problems. By examining the influence of anomie on these behaviors, sociologists can develop strategies to address the underlying social factors that contribute to deviance.

In conclusion, Durkheim's theory of anomie has had a profound impact on the field of sociology, particularly in the study of deviant behavior. By highlighting the relationship between social integration, normlessness, and deviance, Durkheim's theory provides valuable insights into the societal factors that influence individuals' engagement in deviant behaviors. Understanding and addressing anomie can help create more cohesive and supportive societies, reducing the prevalence of deviant behavior and promoting overall well-being.

Deviant Behavior in Different Time Periods

Understanding deviant behavior is a crucial aspect of studying sociology. It helps us gain insights into the complexities of human behavior and the influence of societal norms on individuals. Throughout history, deviant behavior has taken various forms, reflecting the changing social, cultural, and political landscapes of different time periods. By examining these variations, we can better comprehend the evolution of deviant behavior and its impact on society.

In ancient civilizations, deviance was often associated with religious beliefs and practices. For example, in ancient Egypt, individuals who challenged the established religious order were considered deviant and faced severe consequences. Similarly, in ancient Greece, deviant behavior was viewed as an affront to the gods and resulted in social ostracism.

During the Middle Ages, deviance was often linked to witchcraft and heresy. Those who deviated from the religious doctrines enforced by the Church were deemed as evil or possessed by the devil. This led to the infamous witch trials and the persecution of individuals whose actions challenged the prevailing religious authority.

In more recent history, deviant behavior has been influenced by industrialization, urbanization, and the rise of capitalism. The emergence of slums and overcrowded cities during the Industrial Revolution created an environment conducive to deviant behavior, such as theft, prostitution, and substance abuse. Additionally, the social inequalities brought about by capitalism led to the rise of organized crime and white-collar deviance.

The 20th century witnessed a significant transformation in deviant behavior, driven by cultural shifts and technological advancements. The counterculture movements of the 1960s challenged traditional norms and values, resulting in the acceptance of previously deviant behaviors like drug use and unconventional sexual practices.

Today, deviant behavior continues to evolve in response to globalization, technological advancements, and changing social norms. The rise of cybercrime, online harassment, and identity theft can be attributed to the digital age we live in. Furthermore, issues like terrorism, hate crimes, and social media addiction have gained prominence in the 21st century, reflecting the complex interplay between society and deviance.

By examining deviant behavior across different time periods, we gain a deeper understanding of the contextual nature of deviance and its relationship with societal norms. As students of sociology, it is crucial to recognize that deviant behavior is not static, but an ever-changing phenomenon influenced by historical, cultural, and social factors. By studying these variations, we can better comprehend the complexities of human behavior and contribute to the development of effective strategies for addressing deviance in contemporary society.

Chapter 3: Types of Deviant Behavior

Criminal Deviance

In the vast realm of deviant behavior, criminal deviance stands as a prominent and captivating subject of study. As students of sociology, it is crucial to explore this captivating subchapter titled "Criminal Deviance" to gain a comprehensive understanding of the various dimensions of deviant behavior within our society.

Criminal deviance encompasses a broad array of illegal activities that violate the established laws and norms of a society. This subchapter will delve into the causes, consequences, and the sociological theories that attempt to explain the roots of criminal behavior. By examining the social, psychological, and environmental factors that influence criminal deviance, we can gain valuable insights into the multifaceted nature of this phenomenon.

One of the primary objectives of this subchapter is to provide students with an in-depth understanding of the different types of criminal deviance prevalent in society. From street crimes, such as theft and assault, to white-collar crimes, like fraud and embezzlement, we will explore the diverse manifestations of criminal behavior. Additionally, we will examine organized crime, cybercrime, and terrorism, highlighting their distinctive characteristics and societal implications.

Furthermore, this subchapter will critically evaluate the role of social institutions, such as the family, education, and the criminal justice system, in shaping criminal deviance. By analyzing the impact of these institutions on individuals and communities, we can better comprehend the complex interplay between social structures and criminal behavior.

Sociological theories play a fundamental role in understanding criminal deviance. From the classical theories of Cesare Beccaria and Jeremy Bentham to the contemporary approaches of strain theory, labeling theory, and social learning theory, this subchapter will explore how these theories elucidate the causes and consequences of criminal behavior. By applying these theories to real-life case studies, we can gain valuable insights into the motivations behind criminal acts and the factors that contribute to their persistence.

Ultimately, this subchapter on criminal deviance aims to equip students with a comprehensive understanding of the sociological aspects of deviant behavior within our society. By exploring the causes, consequences, and theories surrounding criminal deviance, students can develop a critical perspective and contribute to the ongoing discourse on how to address and prevent criminal behavior for a safer and more just society.

Juvenile Delinquency

Introduction:
In this subchapter, we will delve into the fascinating and complex world of juvenile delinquency. As students of sociology, it is crucial to understand the various factors that contribute to deviant behavior among young individuals. Juvenile delinquency has long been a topic of interest for sociologists, as it offers insights into the social, economic, and cultural influences that shape the lives of young offenders. By exploring this phenomenon, we can gain a deeper understanding of the root causes and potential solutions for juvenile delinquency.

Definition and Scope:
Juvenile delinquency refers to the criminal behavior exhibited by individuals who are minors, typically between the ages of 10 and 17. These offenses range from minor crimes, such as shoplifting or vandalism, to more serious offenses like assault or drug-related crimes. It is essential to recognize that not all young offenders become lifelong criminals, and many outgrow their delinquent behavior as they transition into adulthood.

Causes of Juvenile Delinquency:
Several factors contribute to the development of juvenile delinquency. The subchapter will explore various sociological theories, including strain theory, social disorganization theory, and differential association theory. We will examine how societal factors, such as poverty, family dysfunction, peer influence, and exposure to violence, can lead young individuals down the path of delinquency.

Additionally, we will discuss the role of schools, media, and community in shaping the behavior of juveniles.

Consequences and Implications: Juvenile delinquency has far-reaching consequences for both the individuals involved and society as a whole. This subchapter will explore the short-term and long-term effects of delinquent behavior on the juvenile offenders, their families, and their communities. We will discuss the impact on educational attainment, employment prospects, mental health, and the likelihood of future criminal behavior. Furthermore, we will examine the challenges faced by the justice system in dealing with juvenile offenders and the potential for rehabilitation and intervention.

Prevention and Intervention Strategies: To address the issue of juvenile delinquency effectively, it is crucial to identify prevention and intervention strategies. This subchapter will provide an overview of various programs and initiatives aimed at preventing delinquency and rehabilitating young offenders. We will discuss the importance of early intervention, community-based programs, mentoring, and educational opportunities. By understanding these strategies, students will gain insights into potential solutions to combat juvenile delinquency and create a safer society for all.

Conclusion:
Juvenile delinquency is a complex issue that requires a multidimensional understanding. By examining the various causes, consequences, and prevention strategies, students can develop a comprehensive perspective on this topic. Sociological studies play a

vital role in shedding light on the social dynamics that contribute to delinquent behavior among young individuals. Armed with this knowledge, students can contribute to the development of effective policies and interventions to address the issue of juvenile delinquency and promote a more just and inclusive society.

White-Collar Crime

White-collar crime refers to non-violent illegal activities committed by individuals or organizations in professional or business settings. This subchapter aims to provide students with an in-depth understanding of white-collar crime, its various forms, and its implications in society. By exploring this topic, students will gain insight into deviant behavior within the context of sociology.

White-collar crime encompasses a wide range of offenses, including fraud, embezzlement, money laundering, bribery, insider trading, and identity theft. Unlike traditional crimes, such as robbery or assault, white-collar crimes are often sophisticated and involve manipulation, deception, and abuse of power. Perpetrators of these crimes are typically individuals in positions of authority, such as executives, professionals, or government officials.

One significant aspect of white-collar crime is its impact on society. While the effects may not be immediately visible or tangible, the consequences can be far-reaching. These crimes can lead to financial losses for individuals, businesses, and even governments. They undermine public trust in institutions and contribute to economic inequality. Understanding the social implications of white-collar crime is essential for students to grasp the broader dynamics of deviant behavior and its consequences.

This subchapter will delve into the theories and explanations surrounding white-collar crime, such as the strain theory, control theory, and differential association theory. It will explore how societal factors, such as cultural norms, organizational structures, and economic pressures, contribute to the occurrence and perpetuation of white-collar crime.

Furthermore, students will be introduced to notable cases of white-collar crime and their impact on society. These case studies will shed light on the complexities and challenges in detecting, prosecuting, and preventing white-collar crimes. The subchapter will also discuss the role of law enforcement agencies, regulatory bodies, and the legal system in addressing these crimes, as well as the ethical dilemmas faced by professionals in the field.

By studying white-collar crime through a sociological lens, students will develop critical thinking skills and a deeper understanding of deviant behavior in a societal context. This knowledge will enable them to analyze the underlying causes and consequences of white-collar crime, as well as explore potential solutions and preventive measures. Ultimately, this subchapter aims to equip students with a comprehensive understanding of white-collar crime as a prominent aspect of deviant behavior within the field of sociology.

Organized Crime

Organized crime is a fascinating and complex aspect of deviant behavior that has captured the attention of sociologists for decades. In this subchapter, we will delve deeper into the intricacies of organized crime, its origins, structure, and effects on society. By understanding the inner workings of organized crime, we can gain valuable insights into the dynamics of deviant behavior.

Organized crime refers to a group or network of individuals who engage in illegal activities, often with a hierarchical structure and specialized roles. The activities of these criminal organizations encompass a wide range of illicit practices such as drug trafficking, human smuggling, money laundering, extortion, and even cybercrime. These criminal enterprises operate covertly, with a strong emphasis on secrecy and loyalty among their members.

One of the key factors contributing to the rise of organized crime is the lure of financial gain. The immense profits associated with illegal activities attract individuals who are willing to take risks and exploit opportunities in the black market. Sociologists have also found that social and economic factors, such as poverty, unemployment, and limited access to legal opportunities, play a significant role in driving people toward organized criminal behavior.

The structure of organized crime is often hierarchical, with a clear division of labor and power. At the top, there is usually a leader, often known as the "boss" or the "godfather," who makes critical decisions and oversees the organization's operations. Below the leader, there are various levels of hierarchy, including captains, soldiers, and associates.

Each member has specific roles and responsibilities, ensuring the smooth functioning of the criminal enterprise.

The impact of organized crime on society cannot be underestimated. It not only undermines the rule of law and erodes societal values but also poses significant public safety risks. The involvement of organized crime in drug trafficking, for example, perpetuates addiction and fuels violence in communities. Additionally, the infiltration of organized crime into legitimate businesses can distort market competition and hinder economic development.

Studying organized crime through a sociological lens allows us to analyze the social and structural factors that contribute to its existence. By understanding the root causes and consequences of organized crime, we can develop more effective strategies to combat it. Sociologists play a crucial role in researching and understanding the complex interplay between criminal organizations, individuals, and society, ultimately aiming to create a safer and more just society.

In conclusion, organized crime is a compelling field of study within sociology that sheds light on the inner workings of criminal organizations. By exploring the origins, structure, and societal impact of organized crime, we can gain a deeper understanding of deviant behavior and work towards addressing its root causes. As students of sociology, it is essential to delve into this subchapter with curiosity and a critical mindset, as it provides valuable insights into the complex world of organized crime.

Sexual Deviance

In the realm of sociology, the study of deviant behavior is crucial for understanding the complexities of human interactions and societal norms. One area that has long captured the interest of researchers and scholars is sexual deviance. This subchapter explores the multifaceted nature of sexual deviance, offering students a glimpse into the world of unconventional sexual behaviors, desires, and identities.

Sexual deviance encompasses a broad spectrum of behaviors that fall outside the boundaries of what is considered socially acceptable or normative. It challenges traditional notions of sexuality, gender roles, and relationships, provoking discussions about power, control, consent, and societal taboos. By examining sexual deviance through a sociological lens, students can gain a deeper understanding of how social structures and cultural norms shape and influence sexual behavior.

This subchapter delves into various forms of sexual deviance, including but not limited to fetishism, sadomasochism, exhibitionism, voyeurism, and paraphilias. It explores the historical and cultural contexts that have contributed to the stigmatization and pathologization of these behaviors, shedding light on how societal attitudes towards sexual deviance have evolved over time.

Additionally, this subchapter examines the concept of sexual orientation and its intersection with sexual deviance. It explores the struggles faced by individuals with non-heteronormative sexual orientations, such as homosexuality, bisexuality, and pansexuality, within a predominantly heteronormative society. Through case studies and real-life examples, students can explore the lived experiences of sexual minorities and the social challenges they encounter.

Furthermore, this subchapter critically analyzes the impact of media, technology, and the internet on sexual deviance. It discusses the role of pornography, online communities, and dating apps in shaping sexual desires and behaviors, as well as the potential consequences of their widespread accessibility.

By engaging with the topic of sexual deviance, students can develop a more nuanced perspective on human sexuality and the social forces that shape it. This subchapter serves as a foundation for further exploration of sexual diversity, consent, and the complexities of sexual identities within the field of sociology. Through critical analysis and open-mindedness, students can contribute to a more inclusive and understanding society that respects and acknowledges the diversity of human sexual expression.

Paraphilias

In the vast field of sociology, one topic that has garnered significant attention is that of paraphilias. Paraphilias refer to a range of sexual behaviors and fantasies that are considered atypical or deviant in society. These behaviors often involve intense sexual arousal towards objects, situations, or individuals that are not typically associated with sexual attraction.

Paraphilias can take various forms, from relatively common ones like voyeurism and exhibitionism to more uncommon ones like zoophilia or necrophilia. It is important to note that not all paraphilic behaviors are illegal or harmful. However, some can cross legal boundaries and lead to harmful consequences for both the individuals involved and society at large.

Understanding paraphilias from a sociological perspective is crucial as it allows us to examine the social and cultural factors that shape these behaviors. Societal norms, values, and taboos play a significant role in defining what is considered normal or deviant in terms of sexual behavior. By studying paraphilias, sociologists aim to shed light on the complex interplay between individual desires and societal norms.

One key aspect of studying paraphilias is examining the social construction of deviance. The concept of deviance refers to behaviors that violate social norms. Paraphilias challenge these norms, and studying them helps us understand how society constructs and enforces these norms. It also raises important questions about the power dynamics that shape what is considered deviant and how these judgments are made.

Moreover, studying paraphilias contributes to our understanding of human sexuality and sexual diversity. By exploring these behaviors, we can challenge the notion of a singular "normal" sexuality and recognize the wide range of desires and fantasies that exist within society. This understanding can help reduce stigma and promote acceptance of sexual diversity.

It is important to approach the study of paraphilias with sensitivity and without judgment. While some behaviors may be considered taboo or shocking, it is essential to remember that sociological research aims to provide objective knowledge and insights into human behavior. By studying paraphilias, we can gain a deeper understanding of the complexities of human sexuality and contribute to the broader field of sociology.

In conclusion, the study of paraphilias is a captivating and important field within sociology. By examining these atypical sexual behaviors, we can gain insights into social constructions of deviance, power dynamics, and sexual diversity. As students of sociology, it is our responsibility to approach this topic with open-mindedness and empathy, seeking to understand rather than judge. Through our exploration of paraphilias, we contribute to the ever-evolving understanding of human behavior in society.

Sexual Assault and Harassment

Sexual assault and harassment are prevalent issues that continue to plague societies worldwide. In this subchapter, we will delve into the complex and multifaceted nature of these deviant behaviors. By exploring their sociological aspects, we aim to provide students with a comprehensive understanding of the underlying causes, consequences, and possible solutions.

Sexual assault refers to any unwanted sexual contact or behavior forced upon an individual without their consent. It encompasses a wide range of acts, including rape, sexual coercion, and molestation. Harassment, on the other hand, involves persistent and unwelcome sexual advances, comments, or behaviors that create a hostile environment for the victim.

One of the key sociological theories used to explain sexual assault and harassment is power dynamics. These behaviors are often rooted in power imbalances, with the perpetrator exerting control and dominance over the victim. By examining the intersectionality of race, gender, and social class, we can understand how power differentials contribute to the higher vulnerability of certain groups, such as women and marginalized communities.

Furthermore, cultural and societal factors play a significant role in shaping attitudes towards sexual assault and harassment. Social norms, media influences, and patriarchal structures perpetuate victim-blaming and the trivialization of these offenses. By analyzing these factors, students will gain insights into how societal attitudes can either perpetuate or challenge these harmful behaviors.

The consequences of sexual assault and harassment extend far beyond the immediate physical and psychological harm suffered by the victims. These acts have long-lasting effects on individuals and communities, leading to increased mental health issues, decreased self-esteem, and hindered social interactions. Understanding the broader impact of these deviant behaviors is crucial in designing effective prevention strategies and support systems for survivors.

In this subchapter, we will also explore the efforts made by various organizations, activists, and policymakers to combat sexual assault and harassment. From legal reforms to awareness campaigns, these initiatives aim to create safer environments and empower victims to speak out against their perpetrators. By examining successful interventions and ongoing challenges, students will be equipped with the knowledge to actively contribute to the prevention and eradication of sexual assault and harassment in their communities.

Overall, this subchapter on sexual assault and harassment provides an in-depth sociological analysis of these deviant behaviors. By understanding their underlying causes, consequences, and potential solutions, students will be better prepared to engage in meaningful discussions and take action against these pervasive issues in our society.

Substance Abuse and Addiction

In the subchapter titled "Substance Abuse and Addiction," we delve into the complex world of deviant behavior surrounding drug abuse and addiction within the framework of sociological studies. This chapter aims to provide students of sociology with a comprehensive understanding of the causes, consequences, and social implications of substance abuse and addiction.

We begin by defining substance abuse and addiction, highlighting the distinction between the two. Substance abuse refers to the excessive and harmful use of drugs or alcohol, while addiction represents a chronic and compulsive dependence on substances. We emphasize that these issues are not merely personal choices but are influenced by social, psychological, and economic factors.

Next, we explore the various theories and perspectives within sociology that help explain the prevalence of substance abuse and addiction. We examine the structural-functionalist perspective, which focuses on how societal norms, values, and institutions contribute to substance abuse. Additionally, we discuss the conflict perspective, which emphasizes the role of power, inequality, and social class in shaping substance abuse patterns. Finally, we touch upon the symbolic interactionist perspective, which explores how social interactions and labeling processes influence individuals' drug use behaviors.

Drawing from empirical research, we discuss the social consequences of substance abuse and addiction. We explore the impact on individuals, families, and communities, highlighting the negative effects on physical and mental health, relationships, and economic stability. Furthermore, we examine the strain on the criminal justice system, healthcare resources, and social welfare programs due to substance abuse-related issues.

To provide a holistic understanding, we also explore the role of society and institutions in addressing substance abuse and addiction. We discuss the effectiveness of prevention and treatment programs, harm reduction strategies, and public policies aimed at reducing drug-related harm. Additionally, we shed light on the stigmatization and discrimination faced by individuals struggling with substance abuse disorders, highlighting the need for social support, empathy, and destigmatization efforts.

Throughout this subchapter, we include case studies, statistical data, and real-life examples to illustrate the various concepts and theories discussed. By providing a sociological lens to the study of substance abuse and addiction, we hope to equip students with the knowledge and tools to analyze, understand, and ultimately contribute to addressing these pervasive social issues.

In conclusion, the subchapter "Substance Abuse and Addiction" in the book "Exploring the Underworld: Deviant Behavior in Sociological Studies for Students" offers a comprehensive exploration of the causes, consequences, and social implications of substance abuse and addiction from a sociological perspective. It aims to inform and engage students of sociology in understanding the complex dynamics surrounding these issues and encourages critical analysis and empathy towards individuals affected by substance abuse and addiction.

Drug Abuse

Introduction:
Drug abuse is a prevalent issue that has been extensively studied in the field of sociology. It is a form of deviant behavior that encompasses the excessive and harmful use of drugs, leading to negative consequences for individuals and society as a whole. This subchapter aims to provide students with a comprehensive understanding of drug abuse from a sociological perspective, exploring its causes, consequences, and the role of society in addressing this problem.

Causes of Drug Abuse:
Drug abuse is a complex phenomenon influenced by various factors. Sociologists argue that individual, social, and structural factors contribute to the development of drug abuse. Individual factors include personal characteristics, such as genetic predisposition, mental health issues, and a desire for self-medication. Social factors encompass peer pressure, socialization processes, and cultural norms that may normalize or glamorize drug use. Structural factors refer to socioeconomic disparities, lack of opportunities, and social inequalities that push individuals towards drug abuse as a coping mechanism.

Consequences of Drug Abuse:
Drug abuse has far-reaching consequences at individual, familial, and societal levels. Individuals who abuse drugs often experience deteriorating physical and mental health, impaired cognitive functioning, and increased risk of accidents and violence. Drug abuse can also strain familial relationships, leading to conflicts, neglect, and even separation. Moreover, drug abuse has economic implications, as

38

it burdens healthcare systems and reduces workforce productivity. Societal consequences include the perpetuation of criminal activities, the spread of diseases through needle sharing, and the destabilization of communities affected by drug-related violence.

Society's   Response:
Addressing drug abuse requires a multifaceted approach involving individuals, communities, and policymakers. Sociologists advocate for a comprehensive strategy that focuses on prevention, treatment, and harm reduction. Prevention efforts involve education programs, community outreach, and the promotion of drug-free environments. Treatment options include rehabilitation programs, counseling, and medical interventions. Harm reduction strategies aim to minimize the negative consequences of drug abuse, such as needle exchange programs and safe consumption sites.

Conclusion:
Understanding drug abuse through a sociological lens is crucial for students studying sociology. By examining the causes, consequences, and societal responses to drug abuse, students can gain a holistic understanding of this deviant behavior. Engaging in this topic not only equips students with theoretical knowledge but also empowers them to contribute to the development of effective strategies and policies aimed at reducing drug abuse and its associated harms in our society.

Alcoholism

Alcoholism is a prevalent issue in societies around the world, and its effects on individuals and communities are far-reaching. In this subchapter, we will explore the phenomenon of alcoholism from a sociological perspective, shedding light on its causes, consequences, and potential solutions. By examining the social factors that contribute to alcoholism, we can better understand the complex nature of this deviant behavior.

One of the key aspects to consider when studying alcoholism is the societal norms and values surrounding alcohol consumption. Societies differ in their attitudes towards alcohol, and these cultural variations play a significant role in shaping individual drinking patterns. For instance, in some cultures, heavy drinking may be more socially acceptable, while in others, it may be considered deviant. Understanding these cultural variations helps us grasp why certain groups may be more susceptible to developing alcoholism.

Another crucial factor in the development of alcoholism is the influence of social networks. Research has shown that individuals who have friends or family members who engage in heavy drinking are more likely to become alcoholics themselves. Peer pressure and the normalization of excessive drinking within social circles can contribute to the formation of problematic drinking habits. Moreover, individuals who lack strong social support systems may turn to alcohol as a coping mechanism for stress or loneliness.

The consequences of alcoholism are not limited to the individual suffering from the disorder. Families, communities, and societies at large are also affected. Alcohol abuse can lead to strained relationships, domestic violence, financial difficulties, and a decline in overall well-being. Moreover, the burden on healthcare systems and the justice system due to alcohol-related incidents is significant. By examining these consequences, we can highlight the need for comprehensive interventions and support systems to address the issue of alcoholism effectively.

In conclusion, alcoholism is a complex and multifaceted issue that demands attention from a sociological perspective. By analyzing the social factors that contribute to the development of alcoholism, we can gain insights into the underlying causes and potential solutions. Understanding the cultural variations, the influence of social networks, and the consequences of alcoholism is crucial in developing effective prevention and intervention strategies. This subchapter aims to provide students of sociology with a comprehensive overview of alcoholism, enabling them to contribute to the ongoing discourse and work towards creating a healthier and more understanding society.

Deviance in Mental Health

In the field of sociology, the concept of deviance refers to behaviors or conditions that violate social norms and expectations. Within the realm of mental health, deviance takes on a unique and complex meaning. This subchapter will delve into the various manifestations of deviance in mental health, exploring how sociological studies can shed light on the subject for students interested in sociology and related fields.

Mental health is a vital aspect of overall well-being, and any deviation from what society perceives as "normal" mental functioning is often stigmatized. The stigma associated with mental illness can lead to social exclusion, discrimination, and even the denial of basic human rights for individuals affected by such conditions. Understanding the sociological implications of deviance in mental health is crucial for students aiming to address these social injustices.

One aspect to consider is the social construction of mental illness. Sociologists argue that mental disorders are not objective entities but rather socially constructed categories. The definitions of mental illnesses, their symptoms, and their treatments are influenced by societal norms, values, and power dynamics. By examining the social forces that shape mental health diagnoses, students can gain insights into how deviance is constructed and the implications it has for individuals and society.

Furthermore, sociologists explore how social institutions such as the healthcare system, criminal justice system, and educational institutions respond to deviant behaviors associated with mental health. The overrepresentation of individuals with mental illnesses in the criminal justice system, for example, highlights the need for an understanding of how deviance in mental health intersects with other social issues, such as poverty, race, and gender.

Moreover, this subchapter will also explore the role of social movements and advocacy in challenging the stigmatization of mental illness. Students will learn about the efforts made by various organizations and individuals to promote awareness, destigmatization, and access to mental health services. By understanding the sociological aspects of deviance in mental health, students can contribute to these efforts, fostering inclusive and supportive communities for individuals affected by mental illness.

In conclusion, this subchapter on deviance in mental health provides students with a comprehensive understanding of the sociological implications of mental illness and deviant behaviors. By examining how mental health deviance is constructed, the responses of social institutions, and the role of advocacy, students will gain valuable insights into the complexities of mental health in society. This knowledge will enable students to contribute to the field of sociology and work towards creating a more inclusive and empathetic society.

Personality Disorders

In our study of deviant behavior, it is crucial to examine the fascinating and often complex world of personality disorders. These disorders, characterized by enduring patterns of behavior, cognition, and inner experience, can significantly impact individuals' lives and relationships. Understanding personality disorders from a sociological perspective allows us to explore the social and cultural factors that contribute to their development and manifestation.

One of the most common personality disorders is borderline personality disorder (BPD). People with BPD often struggle with intense and unstable relationships, impulsive behavior, and a distorted self-image. From a sociological standpoint, studying BPD reveals how social interactions, family dynamics, and societal expectations can shape an individual's emotional and behavioral responses.

Another personality disorder that warrants attention is narcissistic personality disorder (NPD). Individuals with NPD tend to exhibit a grandiose sense of self-importance, a constant need for admiration, and a lack of empathy for others. Through a sociological lens, we can explore the cultural influences that perpetuate narcissistic traits, such as societal emphasis on individual success and achievement.

Antisocial personality disorder (ASPD) is another disorder that merits examination. People with ASPD often display a disregard for others' rights and a tendency towards manipulative and exploitative behavior. By analyzing this disorder sociologically, we can delve into the influence of socialization, family dynamics, and broader societal factors on the development of antisocial tendencies.

The study of personality disorders also highlights the intersection between mental health and social institutions. Societal responses to individuals with personality disorders, such as the criminal justice system or mental health services, play a vital role in shaping outcomes for those affected. Analyzing the ways in which society responds to and stigmatizes individuals with personality disorders provides valuable insights into the broader social implications of these conditions.

Furthermore, exploring the relationship between personality disorders and social inequality is crucial. Research has shown that individuals from marginalized backgrounds are disproportionately affected by personality disorders. By examining the ways in which social inequalities contribute to the development and perpetuation of personality disorders, we can work towards creating a more inclusive and equitable society.

In conclusion, studying personality disorders from a sociological perspective allows us to understand the complex interplay between individual experiences and broader social contexts. By exploring the social and cultural factors that contribute to the development and manifestation of personality disorders, we can gain valuable insights into the impact of social interactions, societal expectations, and social inequalities. As students of sociology, delving into the world of personality disorders expands our understanding of deviant behavior and helps us work towards a more compassionate and inclusive society.

Psychopathy

Psychopathy is a fascinating and complex topic that has captivated the field of sociology for many years. This subchapter delves into the intricate world of psychopathy, examining its origins, characteristics, and the impact it has on society. As students of sociology, it is crucial to understand the nuances of deviant behavior, and psychopathy is undoubtedly one of the most intriguing areas to explore.

Psychopathy is a personality disorder characterized by a lack of empathy, remorse, and a disregard for societal norms. It is essential to note that not all individuals with psychopathic traits engage in criminal behavior, but their unique psychological makeup does make them more prone to manipulative and antisocial behaviors. Researchers have long debated the origins of psychopathy, with some arguing that it is primarily a result of genetic factors, while others emphasize the role of environmental influences such as childhood trauma or neglect.

Understanding the characteristics of psychopathy is crucial for sociologists as it helps us identify and study individuals who may pose a risk to society. Traits such as superficial charm, grandiosity, and a propensity for deceit are common among psychopaths. They often excel at manipulating others, using charm and charisma to exploit those around them for personal gain. This ability to deceive and manipulate makes it challenging to detect psychopathy, as they can blend seamlessly into society while secretly wreaking havoc.

The impact of psychopathy on society cannot be understated. Psychopaths often engage in criminal activities, from fraud and white-collar crimes to more violent acts such as murder. Understanding the underlying factors that contribute to psychopathy can help us develop interventions and preventive measures to protect individuals from falling victim to their manipulative tactics.

Moreover, studying psychopathy can shed light on the larger sociological issues of power, control, and inequality within our society. By examining the social, economic, and cultural factors that contribute to the development of psychopathy, we can gain valuable insights into the dynamics of deviant behavior and its broader implications for social order.

In conclusion, psychopathy is a captivating and essential topic in the field of sociology. By exploring the origins, characteristics, and impact of psychopathy on society, we can gain a deeper understanding of deviant behavior and its implications for our social fabric. As students of sociology, delving into the world of psychopathy equips us with the knowledge and tools necessary to analyze and address the complex issues surrounding deviance in our society.

Chapter 4: The Social Construction of Deviance

Labeling Theory

Labeling Theory: Understanding the Power of Social Labels

In the world of sociology, there is a theory that sheds light on the profound impact labels can have on individuals and their behavior. This theory, known as Labeling Theory, explores how society's judgments and stigmas can shape and even create deviant behavior. In this subchapter, we will delve into the depths of Labeling Theory and its implications for understanding deviant behavior in society.

Labeling Theory suggests that deviant behavior is not inherent in individuals, but rather a result of the labels society attaches to certain actions or individuals. These labels, such as "criminal," "addict," or "delinquent," not only influence how society perceives individuals but also how individuals perceive themselves. Once an individual is labeled as deviant, they often internalize this label, leading to a self-fulfilling prophecy where they conform to the expectations set by society.

One of the key concepts of Labeling Theory is the notion of primary and secondary deviance. Primary deviance refers to the initial act of deviance, which may be minor and sporadic. However, when individuals are labeled as deviant, they may experience social rejection, isolation, or even criminalization. This, in turn, can lead to secondary deviance, where individuals fully embrace their deviant identity and engage in continuous deviant behavior as a response to societal labeling.

Moreover, Labeling Theory highlights the importance of social control agencies, such as the police, courts, and media, in perpetuating deviant behavior. These agencies often disproportionately target certain groups, such as minority communities or individuals from lower socioeconomic backgrounds, reinforcing negative labels and further marginalizing these individuals. The theory also emphasizes the role of power dynamics, as labeling often reflects and perpetuates existing social inequalities.

Understanding Labeling Theory is crucial for students of sociology as it challenges traditional notions of deviance and crime. Rather than focusing solely on the individual's actions, this theory encourages us to examine the social processes that contribute to deviant behavior. By recognizing the power of labels, we can better understand how societal reactions to deviance can perpetuate cycles of marginalization and stigmatization.

In conclusion, Labeling Theory provides a fresh perspective on deviant behavior by emphasizing the role of social labels and their impact on individuals and society. It prompts us to critically analyze the mechanisms through which labels are assigned and how they shape individual lives. By studying this theory, students of sociology gain valuable insights into the complexities of deviant behavior and the importance of social context in understanding and addressing these issues.

Social Control and Deviance

In the realm of sociology, understanding social control and deviance is crucial for comprehending the complexities of human behavior and its impact on society. Deviance refers to any behavior or action that violates social norms, which can vary across different cultures and societies. Exploring the concept of deviance allows us to delve into the underlying causes and consequences of non-conforming behavior.

One fundamental aspect of deviance is social control, which encompasses the mechanisms and techniques employed by society to maintain order and conformity. It involves various institutions such as family, education, religion, and the legal system, which collectively aim to shape and regulate individuals' behavior. By enforcing social norms and values, social control ensures that individuals adhere to the accepted standards of conduct within their respective communities.

The study of social control and deviance allows students of sociology to examine the intricate relationship between societal expectations and individual behavior. Sociologists seek to understand why certain behaviors are deemed deviant while others are considered acceptable. Furthermore, they explore how individuals navigate the boundaries of deviance and the consequences they face for violating social norms.

One theory often utilized in the study of deviance is labeling theory. This theory suggests that individuals become deviant when they are labeled as such by society. The label can lead to a self-fulfilling prophecy, where individuals internalize the deviant identity and continue engaging in non-conforming behavior. Labeling theory emphasizes the role of societal reactions in shaping deviant behavior and highlights the potential for social control mechanisms to perpetuate deviance.

Additionally, the subchapter will delve into various forms of deviance, ranging from minor infractions to more serious offenses. It will explore the social construction of deviant behavior, emphasizing the role of power dynamics and social inequalities. Students will be introduced to concepts such as white-collar crime, juvenile delinquency, and drug abuse, providing them with a comprehensive understanding of the multifaceted nature of deviance in contemporary society.

By studying social control and deviance, students will gain critical insights into the mechanisms that shape social order and the consequences of non-conforming behavior. Understanding the dynamics of deviance allows for a more nuanced understanding of societal norms and values, enabling students to critically analyze the complexities of human behavior within different social contexts. This subchapter aims to equip students with the tools necessary to navigate the intricate web of social control and deviance in their future sociological studies.

Deviant Subcultures and Countercultures

In the complex tapestry of human society, various groups emerge that challenge the norms and values upheld by the majority. These groups, known as deviant subcultures and countercultures, play a significant role in the study of sociology. Understanding these phenomena is crucial for students of sociology, as it sheds light on the dynamics of social behavior and the diverse ways individuals navigate societal boundaries.

Deviant subcultures can be defined as smaller groups or communities within society that embrace beliefs, values, and practices that deviate from the dominant culture. These subcultures may form due to shared interests, experiences, or a desire for identity and belonging. Examples of deviant subcultures include punk, goth, and hippie communities, each with their own distinctive styles, ideologies, and norms.

Countercultures, on the other hand, go a step further by actively opposing and challenging the dominant culture. Countercultural movements often emerge in response to social injustices, political ideologies, or cultural hegemony. They seek to create alternative systems and values that challenge the status quo. The countercultural movements of the 1960s, such as the civil rights movement, anti-war protests, and the feminist movement, are prime examples of countercultures that sparked significant social change.

Studying deviant subcultures and countercultures allows students of sociology to delve into the complexities of social identity, resistance, and social change. It provides an opportunity to explore the power dynamics between dominant and marginalized groups, as well as the role of social institutions in maintaining or challenging these dynamics.

By studying deviant subcultures and countercultures, students gain insight into the diverse ways individuals resist social norms and expectations. They learn to question the arbitrary nature of societal boundaries and reflect on the impact of social labeling and stigma on marginalized groups. Additionally, understanding these subcultures can offer a fresh perspective on cultural diversity and the ways in which social change can be initiated and achieved.

In conclusion, the study of deviant subcultures and countercultures is an essential component of sociological exploration. By delving into the intricacies of these phenomena, students of sociology gain valuable insights into social identity, resistance, power dynamics, and social change. Understanding the nuances of deviant subcultures and countercultures helps to cultivate a deeper understanding of human behavior and challenges the notion of a monolithic and homogenous society.

Chapter 5: Deviance and Social Institutions

Deviance in Education

Education is a fundamental aspect of our society, serving as a means to transmit knowledge, skills, and values from one generation to the next. However, like any other social institution, education is not immune to deviant behavior. Deviance in education refers to any behavior or action that violates the established norms and values within the educational setting. Exploring the phenomenon of deviance in education allows us to gain a deeper understanding of the underlying social dynamics and challenges within this important institution.

One prominent form of deviance in education is academic dishonesty. This includes plagiarism, cheating on exams, and fabricating research findings. The pressure to excel academically, coupled with the intense competition among students, can lead to unethical practices. This behavior not only undermines the integrity of the educational system but also hinders the development of critical thinking and problem-solving skills.

Another form of deviance in education is school violence. Incidents such as bullying, physical assaults, and even school shootings are a growing concern in many educational institutions. These acts of deviance not only jeopardize the safety and well-being of students and teachers but also create an environment of fear and anxiety that hinders the learning process.

Deviance in education can also take the form of teacher misconduct. This includes inappropriate relationships with students, favoritism, and abuse of power. Such behavior not only compromises the trust and respect that students should have for their educators but also has long-lasting negative effects on the emotional and psychological well-being of the students involved.

Furthermore, the unequal distribution of educational resources and opportunities can be considered deviant in the context of education. Educational disparities based on socioeconomic status, race, or gender can perpetuate social inequalities and hinder social mobility. This form of deviance challenges the principles of equal access to education and perpetuates systemic injustices.

Understanding deviance in education requires a sociological lens that explores the underlying social structures, power dynamics, and cultural norms within educational institutions. By analyzing the causes and consequences of deviant behavior in education, we can develop strategies to address these issues effectively. This subchapter aims to provide students with a comprehensive overview of deviance in education, encouraging critical thinking and promoting discussions on how to create a more inclusive and equitable educational environment.

Deviance in the Workplace

Introduction:

The workplace, often considered a space of order and conformity, is not immune to deviant behavior. Deviance in the workplace refers to any behavior that violates established norms and expectations, and it can take various forms, ranging from minor transgressions to serious offenses. Understanding deviance in the workplace is crucial for students of sociology as it sheds light on the complexities of human behavior within an organizational setting. This subchapter explores the concept of deviance in the workplace, its causes, and its consequences.

Understanding Deviance in the Workplace:

Deviance in the workplace can manifest in different ways, such as theft, dishonesty, workplace bullying, sexual harassment, absenteeism, substance abuse, and even sabotage. These deviant behaviors can disrupt the functioning of organizations, affect employee morale, and hinder productivity. By studying workplace deviance, students can gain insight into how social factors, organizational culture, and individual motivations contribute to deviant behavior.

Causes of Workplace Deviance:

Several factors contribute to deviance in the workplace. Sociological theories suggest that strain, relative deprivation, and social learning play significant roles in shaping deviant behavior. For instance, employees experiencing strain due to job dissatisfaction, unfair treatment, or lack of opportunities may resort to deviant acts as a means of venting frustration or gaining control. Similarly, individuals who observe and learn deviant behavior from their peers or superiors are more likely to engage in workplace deviance.

Consequences of Workplace Deviance:

The consequences of workplace deviance are far-reaching. It can lead to decreased employee morale, increased turnover rates, and reduced productivity. Moreover, deviant behavior can create a hostile work environment, negatively impacting the mental and emotional well-being of employees. Additionally, workplace deviance may result in legal issues, damaged reputations, and financial losses for organizations.

Preventing and Managing Workplace Deviance:

Understanding and addressing workplace deviance is crucial for organizations to maintain a healthy work environment. This subchapter will explore strategies for preventing and managing workplace deviance, including establishing clear workplace policies, promoting ethical behavior, fostering a positive organizational culture, and implementing effective conflict resolution mechanisms. By studying these strategies, sociology students can develop a comprehensive understanding of how organizations can mitigate deviant behavior and create a more harmonious workplace.

Conclusion:

Deviance in the workplace is a complex phenomenon that requires the attention of sociology students. By exploring the causes and consequences of workplace deviance, students can gain insights into the dynamics of human behavior within organizations. This subchapter aims to equip students with the knowledge and tools needed to understand, prevent, and manage deviant behavior in the workplace, ultimately contributing to the creation of healthier and more productive work environments.

Deviance in Politics and Government

Politics and government are essential components of any society, serving as the backbone of governance and decision-making. However, just like any other social institution, they are not immune to deviant behavior. In this subchapter, we will delve into the intriguing world of deviance in politics and government, exploring the various forms it takes, its causes, and the consequences it has on society.

Deviance in politics can manifest in numerous ways, ranging from corruption and bribery to abuse of power and political scandals. These deviant practices not only erode public trust in the political system but also undermine the democratic principles upon which governments are built. Understanding the dynamics of deviance in politics is crucial for sociologists, as it sheds light on the power struggles, inequalities, and ethical dilemmas that shape our societies.

One of the primary reasons for deviance in politics is the quest for personal gain and power. Many politicians and government officials succumb to the allure of corruption, using their positions for personal enrichment rather than serving the public interest. This unethical behavior not only diverts resources from crucial social programs but also perpetuates a culture of dishonesty and moral decay in politics.

Deviance in politics can also be fueled by systemic factors such as weak institutional frameworks, lack of transparency, and limited accountability mechanisms. When these conditions are present, politicians may feel emboldened to engage in deviant behavior, knowing that they are less likely to face consequences for their actions. Understanding these structural factors is vital for developing effective strategies to combat deviance in politics and strengthen democratic processes.

The consequences of deviance in politics are far-reaching and impact society at large. When politicians engage in corrupt practices or abuse their power, it erodes public trust, leading to disillusionment and apathy among the citizenry. Moreover, deviant behavior in politics can perpetuate social inequalities, as resources are often misallocated, benefiting the few at the expense of the many.

As students of sociology, it is essential to critically analyze the deviant behavior in politics and government. By doing so, we can gain a deeper understanding of the power dynamics at play, the structural factors that contribute to deviance, and the impact it has on society. Armed with this knowledge, we can actively contribute to creating a more transparent, accountable, and just political system that serves the interests of all citizens.

Chapter 6: Deviance and Social Inequality

Class and Deviant Behavior

Subchapter: Class and Deviant Behavior

Introduction:

In the study of deviant behavior, one cannot neglect the crucial role that social class plays in shaping individuals' actions and choices. This subchapter explores the intricate relationship between class and deviant behavior, shedding light on how social stratification influences the likelihood of engaging in deviant acts. By examining various sociological perspectives and empirical evidence, we aim to deepen our understanding of the complex dynamics between class and deviance.

Social Class and Deviance:

Social class refers to the hierarchical division of society into distinct groups based on economic, occupational, and educational factors. Deviant behavior, on the other hand, encompasses actions that deviate from societal norms and values. While deviance can occur across all classes, the relationship between class and deviant behavior is far from uniform.

The Linkages:

One perspective exploring the link between class and deviance is the strain theory. According to this theory, individuals from lower social classes often face strains and frustrations due to limited opportunities for upward mobility. As a result, they are more likely to engage in deviant behavior as a means of achieving their goals or venting their frustrations.

Another perspective is the labeling theory, which suggests that individuals from lower classes are more likely to be labeled as deviant by the dominant class. This labeling not only reinforces their marginalized position but also increases the likelihood of further deviant behavior due to the stigmatization they experience.

Empirical Evidence:

Numerous studies have examined the connection between social class and deviant behavior. For instance, research has shown that individuals from lower social classes are disproportionately represented in crime statistics. Factors such as limited access to quality education, high unemployment rates, and economic inequality contribute to this disparity.

Furthermore, the study of white-collar crime highlights how individuals from higher social classes may engage in deviant behavior that often goes unnoticed or unpunished due to their privileged position. This highlights the importance of considering class when analyzing deviance.

Conclusion:

Understanding the relationship between social class and deviant behavior is essential for comprehending the broader social dynamics at play. By recognizing the influence of social stratification on deviant behavior, we can develop more comprehensive strategies to address the root causes of deviance. As students of sociology, it is crucial to critically examine the role of class in shaping deviant behavior and work towards creating a more equitable society where opportunities and resources are accessible to all.

Race and Deviant Behavior

In the multifaceted realm of deviant behavior, the interplay between race and societal norms is a complex and contentious issue. The study of how race intersects with deviant behavior is an essential aspect of sociological studies, shedding light on the dynamics of power, inequality, and social control within a given society. This subchapter delves into the intricate relationship between race and deviant behavior, examining its historical roots, contemporary manifestations, and the social implications it carries.

To comprehend the association between race and deviant behavior, it is crucial to understand the historical context in which these dynamics unfolded. From colonialism to slavery, racial discrimination has shaped societal structures and power dynamics, leading to a disproportionate representation of certain racial groups in deviant behaviors. The chapter explores how racial stereotyping, prejudice, and discrimination have contributed to the marginalization and stigmatization of certain racial communities, thereby influencing their likelihood to engage in deviant acts.

Furthermore, this subchapter delves into the contemporary manifestations of race and deviant behavior. It critically examines the over-policing and racial profiling practices that contribute to the criminalization of specific racial groups. Drawing from extensive research, it discusses how racial disparities in the criminal justice system perpetuate social inequalities, highlighting the disproportionate rates of arrest, conviction, and incarceration among marginalized racial communities. The subchapter also explores how the experience of racial discrimination and social exclusion can lead individuals to adopt deviant behaviors as a form of resistance or survival mechanism.

Beyond examining the correlation between race and deviant behavior, this subchapter also explores the broader social implications of these dynamics. By analyzing the impact of racialized deviant behavior on community dynamics, the chapter highlights the perpetuation of stereotypes, the formation and reinforcement of racial prejudices, and the perpetuation of social inequalities. It also emphasizes the importance of adopting a holistic approach that considers the interconnectedness of race, class, and gender in understanding deviant behavior.

In sum, this subchapter provides an in-depth analysis of the intricate relationship between race and deviant behavior. It serves as a valuable resource for sociology students, offering critical insights into the historical roots, contemporary manifestations, and social implications of this complex dynamic. By understanding the interplay between race and deviant behavior, students will be better equipped to engage with the sociological perspectives needed to address and challenge the racial disparities and injustices prevalent in society today.

Gender and Deviant Behavior

In the study of deviant behavior, it is crucial to explore the influence of gender. Gender plays a significant role in shaping societal norms, expectations, and the ways in which individuals navigate their environment. Understanding the relationship between gender and deviance is crucial for students of sociology, as it sheds light on the complexities of social dynamics and the ways in which individuals both conform to and challenge societal norms.

Sociological research consistently highlights the gendered nature of deviant behavior. While both men and women engage in deviant acts, the types of deviance they exhibit often differ. For example, studies have shown that men are more likely to engage in criminal activities such as theft, assault, and drug trafficking. On the other hand, women are more likely to engage in non-violent forms of deviance, such as prostitution, shoplifting, or substance abuse. These gendered patterns of deviance can be attributed to a variety of factors, including societal expectations, cultural norms, and access to resources.

One explanation for the gender differences in deviance is the socialization process. From an early age, boys and girls are socialized differently, with boys often encouraged to be assertive, competitive, and risk-taking, while girls are encouraged to be nurturing, compliant, and risk-averse. These gendered expectations can influence the types of deviant behavior individuals engage in. For example, the pressure on men to be dominant and aggressive may lead to their involvement in violent crimes, while the societal constraints on women may limit their opportunities for engaging in certain types of deviance.

Moreover, the link between gender and deviance is also influenced by power dynamics. In many societies, men hold more power and privilege than women, which can impact the types of deviant behavior they engage in. For instance, men may have greater access to resources that enable them to engage in white-collar crimes, such as embezzlement or fraud, while women may resort to alternative forms of deviance due to limited opportunities for financial gain.

By studying gender and deviant behavior, students of sociology gain a deeper understanding of the complexities of social norms, power dynamics, and the ways in which individuals navigate societal expectations. Recognizing the gendered patterns of deviance is crucial for developing effective strategies for prevention and intervention. Furthermore, examining gender and deviance helps challenge traditional notions of masculinity and femininity and encourages a more nuanced understanding of human behavior.

In conclusion, the subchapter on "Gender and Deviant Behavior" provides students of sociology with invaluable insights into the relationship between gender and deviance. By exploring the gendered patterns of deviant behavior, students can better comprehend the social dynamics that shape our world. This knowledge is essential for developing a comprehensive understanding of deviance and its impact on individuals and society as a whole.

Chapter 7: Deviant Behavior and Technology

Cyberbullying and Online Harassment

In today's digital age, where connectivity and communication are at their peak, the dark side of the internet has become a growing concern. Cyberbullying and online harassment are two forms of deviant behavior that have emerged from the advent of technology and the widespread use of social media platforms. This subchapter aims to explore the nature and consequences of cyberbullying and online harassment, shedding light on their sociological implications.

Cyberbullying refers to the deliberate and repeated use of digital communication tools to harass, intimidate, or harm others. Unlike traditional bullying, cyberbullying takes place in the virtual realm, making it harder to escape and potentially more damaging. With the anonymity provided by the internet, individuals engage in cyberbullying without facing immediate consequences, resulting in an increase in the frequency and intensity of these acts.

Online harassment, on the other hand, encompasses a broader range of behaviors that aim to intimidate, threaten, or torment individuals online. This can include sending hate messages, spreading rumors, doxing (revealing personal information), or engaging in online stalking. Such acts not only violate the privacy and safety of the victims but also have serious psychological and emotional repercussions.

From a sociological perspective, cyberbullying and online harassment can be understood as reflections of power dynamics within society. They often occur within existing social hierarchies, where individuals seek to assert dominance or control over others. The anonymity offered by the internet allows perpetrators to act without accountability, further perpetuating power imbalances.

Moreover, the impact of cyberbullying and online harassment extends beyond individual victims. These behaviors can lead to the formation of online communities that thrive on negativity and cruelty, creating a toxic online environment. The ripple effect of such behavior can contribute to a culture of fear, anxiety, and even depression among internet users.

To combat cyberbullying and online harassment, it is essential to raise awareness and promote digital literacy among students. Understanding the consequences of these behaviors and the ethical implications of online actions is crucial for developing a responsible and compassionate online community. Sociological studies play a vital role in identifying the underlying causes and patterns of cyberbullying and online harassment, providing insights for interventions and policies that can help mitigate these issues.

In conclusion, cyberbullying and online harassment have emerged as significant challenges in our increasingly digital world. By studying these phenomena through a sociological lens, students can gain a deeper understanding of the social dynamics and power structures that contribute to these behaviors. By fostering empathy and promoting digital citizenship, we can strive towards creating a safer and more inclusive online environment for all.

Deviant Behavior in Gaming Communities

In recent years, gaming has emerged as a popular form of entertainment, connecting millions of individuals worldwide through virtual landscapes and interactive experiences. However, within these seemingly harmless gaming communities, a darker side often lurks. Deviant behavior in gaming communities has become a topic of great interest in sociological studies, shedding light on the various forms of misconduct, rule-breaking, and social disruption that occur within these virtual spaces.

One of the most prevalent forms of deviant behavior in gaming communities is cheating. Whether through the use of hacking tools, exploiting glitches, or colluding with other players, cheaters undermine the integrity of the game and create an unfair advantage for themselves. This not only disrupts the gameplay experience for others but also challenges the norms and rules established by the gaming community.

Another form of deviance that arises within gaming communities is toxic behavior. This includes engaging in verbal abuse, harassment, or trolling other players. The anonymity provided by online gaming platforms often emboldens individuals to unleash their worst tendencies, resulting in a hostile and toxic environment for others. Such behavior not only affects the mental well-being of players but also hinders the formation of positive social interactions within the gaming community.

Furthermore, the phenomenon of griefing is another aspect of deviant behavior prevalent in gaming communities. Griefers intentionally disrupt the gameplay experience of others, often by repeatedly attacking or sabotaging their progress. This disruptive behavior serves as a means of exerting power and control over others, highlighting the complex dynamics of social power within gaming communities.

The consequences of deviant behavior in gaming communities extend beyond the virtual realm. Research suggests that individuals who engage in deviant behavior while gaming are more likely to exhibit similar patterns of misconduct in their offline lives. This raises important questions about the impact of virtual experiences on individuals' behavior and the potential for gaming communities to serve as breeding grounds for deviant behavior.

Understanding deviant behavior in gaming communities is crucial not only for sociological studies but also for the development of strategies to mitigate and prevent such behavior. By examining the underlying motives, social dynamics, and consequences of deviant behavior, sociologists can provide valuable insights into effective interventions and policies that promote healthier and more inclusive gaming communities.

In conclusion, deviant behavior in gaming communities is a multifaceted topic that deserves careful examination. From cheating and toxic behavior to griefing, the deviant tendencies that emerge within these virtual spaces have significant implications for individuals and society at large. By exploring and understanding these behaviors, students of sociology can contribute to the development of a more empathetic and harmonious gaming environment, where individuals can enjoy their virtual experiences without fear of harassment or disruption.

Deviance in the Dark Web

The Dark Web, a hidden realm of the internet that is inaccessible through regular search engines, has become a subject of great fascination and concern in recent years. It is a space where anonymity reigns supreme, making it an attractive platform for deviant behavior. In this subchapter, we will delve into the world of deviance in the Dark Web, exploring its unique characteristics and the sociological implications it holds.

To understand deviance in the Dark Web, it is crucial to grasp the concept of deviant behavior itself. Deviance refers to any behavior that goes against societal norms and expectations. The Dark Web provides a breeding ground for deviance due to its lack of regulation and the ability to maintain anonymity. It is an environment where illegal activities, such as drug trafficking, human trafficking, hacking, and identity theft, can flourish without fear of detection or consequences.

Sociologically, the Dark Web presents a fascinating case study in understanding the factors that contribute to deviant behavior. It raises questions about the role of anonymity, the impact of social structures, and the influence of technology on deviance. By studying the Dark Web, sociologists can gain valuable insights into the motivations and dynamics of deviant individuals and groups.

Moreover, exploring deviance in the Dark Web allows us to critically analyze the broader implications for society. The Dark Web challenges traditional notions of law and order and forces us to question the efficacy of our legal systems in combating deviant behavior online. It also sheds light on the power dynamics and inequalities that exist in the digital realm, as well as the ethical dilemmas surrounding privacy and surveillance.

For students of sociology, studying deviance in the Dark Web opens doors to a deeper understanding of deviant behavior and its social implications. It provides an opportunity to critically examine the interplay between technology, society, and deviance, ultimately contributing to a more comprehensive sociological understanding of the world we live in.

In conclusion, the Dark Web serves as a unique and intriguing arena for deviant behavior. By exploring the deviance that occurs within this hidden realm, students of sociology can gain valuable insights into the motivations, dynamics, and societal implications of deviant behavior. The study of deviance in the Dark Web provides an opportunity to critically analyze the complex relationship between technology, society, and deviance, contributing to a deeper understanding of the underbelly of our digital world.

Chapter 8: Consequences of Deviant Behavior

Stigma and Social Exclusion

In the realm of sociology, the notions of stigma and social exclusion play a crucial role in understanding deviant behavior within society. This subchapter aims to delve into the intricacies of these concepts, shedding light on their impact on individuals and communities.

Stigma, as defined by sociologist Erving Goffman, refers to a mark of disgrace or discredit that sets an individual apart from others. It is often associated with deviant behaviors, physical or mental disabilities, and other characteristics that deviate from societal norms. Stigmatized individuals are subjected to negative stereotypes and prejudices, which can lead to social exclusion and discrimination.

Stigmatization can be both overt and subtle, occurring at different levels of interaction. For instance, an individual with a criminal record might face overt stigma in the form of rejection from potential employers. On the other hand, someone with a mental health condition might experience subtle stigma through the use of derogatory language or avoidance by acquaintances.

Social exclusion refers to the process of marginalizing individuals or groups from participating fully in social activities, leading to their alienation from society. This exclusion can be intentional or unintentional, resulting from various factors such as race, ethnicity, gender, socioeconomic status, or even physical appearance.

The consequences of stigma and social exclusion can be far-reaching, affecting an individual's self-esteem, mental health, and overall well-being. Stigmatized individuals often internalize negative societal perceptions, leading to feelings of shame, isolation, and a diminished sense of self-worth. Moreover, social exclusion can limit access to resources, opportunities, and supportive networks, perpetuating a cycle of disadvantage.

It is crucial for students of sociology to understand the mechanisms and effects of stigma and social exclusion to promote social justice and inclusion. By recognizing the power of societal labels and stereotypes, students can challenge prevailing narratives and advocate for equal rights and opportunities for stigmatized individuals.

Exploring strategies for combating stigma and social exclusion is another essential aspect of this subchapter. Students can learn about the importance of education, awareness campaigns, and destigmatization efforts to foster empathy, reduce prejudice, and create inclusive environments. By examining case studies and real-life examples, students can gain a deeper understanding of the complexities surrounding stigma and social exclusion, equipping them with the tools to challenge societal norms and promote positive change.

In conclusion, stigma and social exclusion are integral components of the study of deviant behavior in sociology. Through comprehensive knowledge of these concepts, students can strive to create a more inclusive and accepting society, where everyone is valued and respected irrespective of their differences.

Criminal Justice System and Deviance

Introduction:

In the world we live in, deviant behavior and its consequences are topics that captivate our attention. Understanding how society responds to deviance is crucial for students aspiring to study sociology. This subchapter will delve into the intricate relationship between deviance and the criminal justice system, shedding light on the various approaches and theories sociologists use to analyze these phenomena. By exploring the underpinnings of deviant behavior and how society responds to it, we can gain a deeper understanding of the complexities of the criminal justice system.

Exploring Deviant Behavior:

Deviant behavior refers to actions that stray from societal norms and expectations. In the context of the criminal justice system, deviance often involves acts that are prohibited by law and carry legal consequences. Sociologists study deviance to comprehend its causes, patterns, and the social reactions it elicits. By analyzing deviance, sociologists aim to uncover the mechanisms that shape our legal and social systems.

The Role of the Criminal Justice System:

The criminal justice system plays a pivotal role in responding to deviant behavior. It consists of various institutions, including law enforcement agencies, courts, and correctional facilities. Each institution within the criminal justice system has a specific function, such as investigating crimes, administering justice, and rehabilitating offenders. Sociologists examine how these institutions operate, their effectiveness, and the impact they have on individuals and society.

Theories and Approaches:

Sociologists employ various theories and approaches to understand the criminal justice system's response to deviance. The conflict perspective focuses on the power dynamics between different social groups, emphasizing how the criminal justice system may disproportionately target marginalized communities. The labeling theory explores how the criminal justice system labels individuals as deviant, potentially leading to self-fulfilling prophecies and further criminal behavior. Additionally, the strain theory examines how societal pressures and inequalities can push individuals toward deviance.

Implications and Critiques:

Understanding the criminal justice system's response to deviance raises important questions about fairness, equity, and social control. Sociologists critically examine the potential biases and flaws within the system, such as racial profiling, disparities in sentencing, and the overrepresentation of certain groups within correctional facilities. By identifying these issues, sociologists can advocate for reforms and policies that promote a more just and equitable criminal justice system.

Conclusion:

Exploring the relationship between deviance and the criminal justice system is essential for students studying sociology. This subchapter has provided an overview of deviant behavior, the role of the criminal justice system, and the theories and approaches used by sociologists to analyze these phenomena. By critically examining the criminal justice system's response to deviance, students can gain a deeper understanding of its implications and work toward creating a more equitable society.

Rehabilitation and Reintegration

In the realm of deviant behavior, the process of rehabilitation and reintegration plays a crucial role in understanding and addressing the challenges faced by individuals who have engaged in such behaviors. In this subchapter, we delve into the concept of rehabilitation and reintegration from a sociological perspective, shedding light on its significance and impact on society.

Rehabilitation refers to the process of aiding individuals in overcoming their deviant behaviors and reintegrating them back into society as law-abiding citizens. It recognizes that deviant behavior is often a result of complex social, psychological, and environmental factors. Therefore, instead of merely punishing offenders, the focus shifts towards understanding the root causes of their actions and providing interventions to address these underlying issues.

From a sociological standpoint, rehabilitation acknowledges the role of social structures and institutions in shaping an individual's behavior. It recognizes that factors such as poverty, inequality, and social exclusion can contribute to deviant behavior. By addressing these structural issues, rehabilitation aims to prevent reoffending and create a more inclusive and just society.

Rehabilitation programs encompass a range of interventions, including psychological counseling, skills development, education, and vocational training. These programs are designed to empower individuals, enhance their self-esteem, and equip them with the tools necessary to reintegrate successfully into their communities. By providing support and guidance, rehabilitation programs aim to break the cycle of deviant behavior and facilitate the offender's transition to a law-abiding life.

Reintegration, on the other hand, focuses on the process of incorporating rehabilitated individuals back into society. It recognizes that the successful reintegration of offenders is essential for reducing recidivism rates and promoting social cohesion. Reintegration involves creating a supportive environment that welcomes and accepts individuals who have undergone rehabilitation. This may require efforts from various stakeholders, including families, communities, employers, and the criminal justice system.

Sociology plays a critical role in understanding the broader social implications of rehabilitation and reintegration. By studying the social dynamics surrounding deviant behavior and its consequences, sociologists can contribute valuable insights into the development and implementation of effective rehabilitation programs. They can also shed light on the impact of social structures and policies on the successful reintegration of individuals back into society.

In conclusion, the process of rehabilitation and reintegration is a vital component of addressing deviant behavior from a sociological perspective. It recognizes the multifaceted nature of deviance and seeks to address its underlying causes through comprehensive interventions. By focusing on rehabilitation and reintegration, we can strive towards a more inclusive and just society, where individuals are given the opportunity to rebuild their lives and contribute positively to their communities.

Chapter 9: Researching Deviant Behavior

Quantitative Research Methods

In the field of sociology, research is crucial for understanding and explaining various social phenomena. One approach that researchers employ is quantitative research methods. This subchapter aims to introduce students to the fundamentals of quantitative research methods and their significance in sociological studies.

Quantitative research methods involve the collection and analysis of numerical data to uncover patterns, relationships, and trends within a given population or sample. Unlike qualitative research, which focuses on subjective experiences and in-depth understanding, quantitative research aims to measure and quantify social phenomena using statistical analysis.

One of the key advantages of quantitative research methods is its ability to provide generalizable findings. By collecting data from a representative sample, researchers can make inferences about a larger population. This allows sociologists to gain a broader understanding of social phenomena and make predictions about societal trends.

To conduct quantitative research, researchers often employ surveys, experiments, and secondary data analysis. Surveys involve administering questionnaires to a sample of individuals to collect data on their attitudes, beliefs, behaviors, or demographics. Experiments, on the other hand, involve manipulating variables and measuring their impact on participants' behavior or attitudes. Lastly, secondary data analysis involves analyzing existing datasets collected by other researchers or organizations.

In quantitative research, data is typically collected using structured instruments, such as questionnaires or rating scales, to ensure consistency and comparability. Once the data is collected, it is analyzed using statistical techniques to identify patterns, correlations, and significant differences.

However, it is important for students to recognize the limitations of quantitative research methods. While they provide valuable insights into social phenomena, they often overlook the complexity and nuances of human behavior. Additionally, the reliance on numerical data may oversimplify the social reality, leading to reductionism.

Despite these limitations, quantitative research methods remain a powerful tool in sociology. They allow researchers to examine large-scale social trends, test hypotheses, and provide evidence for policymaking. As students delve deeper into sociological studies, understanding quantitative research methods will equip them with the necessary skills to critically evaluate research findings and contribute to the field.

In conclusion, quantitative research methods play a crucial role in sociological studies. They enable researchers to measure and quantify social phenomena, providing generalizable findings and contributing to the broader understanding of society. By familiarizing themselves with quantitative research methods, students in sociology can enhance their research skills and contribute to the ongoing exploration of deviant behavior and other sociological phenomena.

Qualitative Research Methods

In the field of sociology, researchers employ various methods to gain a deeper understanding of deviant behavior and its underlying causes. One such approach is qualitative research, which focuses on exploring the subjective experiences and perspectives of individuals or groups. This subchapter aims to provide students with an overview of qualitative research methods commonly used in sociological studies.

Qualitative research methods involve collecting and analyzing non-numerical data, such as interviews, observations, and textual analysis. These methods allow researchers to capture the complexity and richness of human behavior, motivations, and social interactions. Through qualitative research, students can gain insights into the social factors that contribute to deviant behavior, as well as the meanings and interpretations individuals assign to these behaviors.

One commonly used qualitative research method is in-depth interviews. Researchers conduct face-to-face or virtual interviews with individuals who have experienced or engaged in deviant behavior. By asking open-ended questions, they encourage participants to share their personal experiences, beliefs, and emotions related to their deviant acts. These interviews provide valuable insights into the motivations, social circumstances, and consequences of deviant behavior, enabling students to understand the social context in which it occurs.

Additionally, observational research allows students to directly observe and document deviant behavior in its natural setting. Researchers may conduct participant observation, immersing themselves in a particular social group or environment to gain a deeper understanding of its norms, values, and deviant practices. This method helps students uncover the social dynamics that contribute to deviant behavior and provides a more comprehensive understanding of the deviant subculture.

Textual analysis is another valuable qualitative research method that involves examining written or visual materials related to deviant behavior. Researchers analyze documents, such as newspaper articles, court records, or online forums, to identify patterns, themes, and discourses surrounding deviant acts. This method helps students understand how deviance is constructed and represented in society, shedding light on the social reactions and perceptions associated with different forms of deviant behavior.

In conclusion, qualitative research methods play a crucial role in sociological studies focused on deviant behavior. By utilizing in-depth interviews, observations, and textual analysis, researchers can delve into the subjective experiences, social factors, and cultural contexts that shape deviance. By employing these methods, students gain a deeper understanding of the complexities surrounding deviant behavior and its implications for society.

Ethical Considerations in Studying Deviance

In the field of sociology, the study of deviance plays a crucial role in understanding the complexities of human behavior and society. Deviance refers to behaviors, actions, or characteristics that violate social norms and are deemed unacceptable within a particular society. However, studying deviance raises a multitude of ethical considerations that researchers must carefully navigate to ensure the protection and well-being of both the subjects and the broader community.

One of the primary ethical considerations in studying deviance is the potential harm it may cause to the individuals being studied. Researchers must be mindful of the potential psychological, emotional, and physical harm that may result from discussing or investigating sensitive topics related to deviance. It is crucial to obtain informed consent from participants, ensuring they are fully aware of the purpose, risks, and benefits of their involvement. Furthermore, researchers must provide support systems and resources to help participants cope with any distress that may arise during or after the study.

Maintaining confidentiality and anonymity is another vital ethical consideration in studying deviance. Participants may be reluctant to share personal information or engage in candid discussions if they fear their identity will be revealed. Researchers must guarantee strict confidentiality and take necessary precautions to protect the privacy of their subjects. This includes using pseudonyms, securely storing data, and ensuring that only authorized personnel have access to the information.

Additionally, researchers must be mindful of the potential stigmatization or unintended consequences that may arise from their findings. The portrayal of deviant behaviors and individuals in research can perpetuate stereotypes, reinforce negative public perceptions, or even lead to discrimination. It is essential for researchers to present their findings in a balanced and unbiased manner, avoiding sensationalism or exaggeration that may harm the reputations or well-being of those being studied.

Finally, ethical considerations also extend to the broader community impacted by the study of deviance. Researchers must consider the potential consequences of their work on society, ensuring that their findings are used for educational purposes and social change rather than further marginalization or harm. It is crucial to engage in responsible dissemination of results and actively contribute to public discourse to promote a better understanding of deviance and foster positive change.

In conclusion, the study of deviance in sociology requires researchers to carefully consider ethical considerations to protect the well-being of both the subjects and the broader community. By obtaining informed consent, ensuring confidentiality, avoiding stigmatization, and promoting responsible dissemination of findings, researchers can contribute to a better understanding of deviance while upholding ethical standards in their work.

Chapter 10: Future Directions in Deviant Behavior Sociology

Emerging Trends in Deviant Behavior

In the ever-changing landscape of society, the study of deviant behavior is crucial in understanding the complex dynamics that shape our world. Deviant behavior refers to any action or behavior that violates social norms and is perceived as different, abnormal, or unacceptable by the majority of society. As students of sociology, it is essential to explore the emerging trends in deviant behavior to gain a comprehensive understanding of the multifaceted nature of human interactions.

One notable emerging trend in deviant behavior is cyberbullying. With the rapid advancement of technology and the widespread use of social media platforms, individuals are now able to engage in harmful and malicious behavior online. Cyberbullying involves the use of electronic communication to intimidate, harass, or harm others, often leading to severe psychological consequences for the victims. Sociology students must delve into the underlying reasons for this trend, such as the anonymity and perceived detachment from consequences that the online world offers.

Another emerging trend in deviant behavior is substance abuse among young adults. While substance abuse has long been a concern in society, the patterns and substances of choice are continually evolving. Today, there is an increasing prevalence of synthetic drugs, designer drugs, and the misuse of prescription medications. Sociologists need to explore the social, economic, and psychological factors that contribute to the rise in substance abuse among young adults to develop effective prevention and intervention strategies.

Furthermore, the phenomenon of "cancel culture" has gained significant attention in recent years. Cancel culture refers to the practice of boycotting or ostracizing individuals, often celebrities or public figures, who have engaged in behavior deemed inappropriate or offensive by a particular group. Sociology students should analyze the societal implications of cancel culture, including its impact on freedom of speech, public discourse, and the dynamics of power and influence.

Lastly, the exploration of deviant behavior must also include an examination of the emerging trend of radicalization and extremism. With the rise of social and political unrest globally, individuals are increasingly susceptible to radical ideologies that promote violence and hatred. Understanding the root causes and processes of radicalization is crucial for sociologists to contribute to the development of effective counter-terrorism strategies and deradicalization programs.

As students of sociology, it is essential to keep a finger on the pulse of emerging trends in deviant behavior. By studying and analyzing these trends, we can gain valuable insights into the social, cultural, and psychological factors that contribute to deviance, and ultimately work towards creating a more inclusive and harmonious society.

The Role of Technology in Shaping Deviance

In today's rapidly advancing technological era, it is imperative to acknowledge the profound impact it has on shaping deviant behavior within our society. The interplay between technology and deviance is a topic of immense significance and relevance in the field of sociology. As students delving into the depths of deviant behavior, it is essential to explore how technology acts as both a catalyst and a facilitator for deviant acts.

One significant aspect of technology's role in shaping deviance is its ability to create new forms of deviant behavior. With the advent of the internet and social media platforms, deviant acts such as cyberbullying, online fraud, and hacking have become prevalent. The anonymity provided by these platforms allows individuals to engage in deviant behavior without the fear of immediate consequences. This newfound anonymity has led to a rise in deviance, as individuals feel emboldened to engage in acts they may not have otherwise committed in face-to-face interactions.

Moreover, technology has also played a crucial role in expanding the reach of deviant behavior. Through the internet, deviant individuals can now connect with like-minded individuals across the globe, forming virtual communities centered around deviance. These communities provide a breeding ground for the exchange of deviant ideas, further normalizing deviant behavior and facilitating its spread. The ease of communication and the ability to disseminate deviant content through technology have amplified the impact of deviance, making it more accessible and influential than ever before.

Additionally, technology has also transformed traditional forms of deviance. For instance, the rise of digital piracy has severely impacted the entertainment industry. The ease of sharing copyrighted material through file-sharing platforms has led to significant financial losses for artists and content creators. This form of deviance challenges the existing legal and ethical framework, blurring the lines between what is deemed acceptable and what is considered deviant.

As students of sociology, it is crucial to critically examine the role of technology in shaping deviant behavior. Understanding the ways in which technology influences and perpetuates deviance can help us develop strategies for prevention and intervention. Through research and analysis, we can gain insights into the underlying factors that contribute to the emergence and sustenance of deviant behavior in the digital age.

In conclusion, technology has become an integral part of our lives, both shaping and being shaped by deviant behavior. The relationship between technology and deviance is complex, with technology acting as a catalyst, facilitator, and transformer of deviant acts. As students exploring the underworld of deviant behavior, it is our responsibility to delve into this relationship, understand its intricacies, and work towards creating a better, more informed society.

Implications for Policy and Intervention

In the realm of sociology, the study of deviant behavior holds immense value in understanding the intricacies of society. Exploring the Underworld: Deviant Behavior in Sociological Studies for Students delves into this fascinating subject, shedding light on the various implications it has for policy and intervention. This subchapter specifically addresses the critical role that policy-making and intervention strategies play in mitigating deviant behavior and creating a harmonious society.

One of the key takeaways from this subchapter is the importance of evidence-based policy-making. Sociological studies provide invaluable insights into the root causes and patterns of deviant behavior, thereby enabling policymakers to devise strategies that effectively address these issues. By incorporating empirical evidence and rigorous research, policymakers can make informed decisions that have a lasting impact on society.

Moreover, this subchapter emphasizes the need for a holistic approach to intervention. While punitive measures have traditionally been the go-to response to deviant behavior, sociological research suggests that a multifaceted approach is more effective. This entails understanding the underlying factors that contribute to deviance, such as social inequality, poverty, and lack of access to education and healthcare. By addressing these root causes, interventions can be tailored to prevent deviant behavior from occurring in the first place.

Furthermore, this subchapter highlights the significance of community-based interventions. Sociological studies have shown that communities play a crucial role in shaping individual behavior. Therefore, empowering communities to actively participate in intervention programs can yield positive outcomes. This can be achieved by fostering a sense of collective responsibility and creating support networks that provide resources and guidance to individuals at risk of engaging in deviant behavior.

In addition, this subchapter stresses the importance of early intervention. Sociological research indicates that deviant behavior often emerges during adolescence, and timely interventions during this critical period can effectively steer individuals away from a path of deviance. By investing in educational programs, mentoring initiatives, and counseling services, policymakers can provide the necessary support and guidance to young individuals, thereby reducing the likelihood of their involvement in deviant activities.

In conclusion, the subchapter on "Implications for Policy and Intervention" in Exploring the Underworld: Deviant Behavior in Sociological Studies for Students underscores the significance of evidence-based policy-making, holistic intervention strategies, community involvement, and early intervention. By incorporating these principles into policy and practice, society can work towards creating a safer, more inclusive, and harmonious environment for all. As students of sociology, it is essential to grasp the implications discussed in this subchapter, as it equips us with the knowledge and tools needed to contribute towards positive social change.

Conclusion: Understanding Deviant Behavior in Sociological Studies

In conclusion, the study of deviant behavior in sociology offers valuable insights into the complexities of human behavior and society. Throughout this book, "Exploring the Underworld: Deviant Behavior in Sociological Studies for Students," we have delved into various aspects of deviance, aiming to provide students with a comprehensive understanding of this fascinating field.

Deviance, as we have learned, refers to any behavior that violates societal norms. It encompasses a wide range of actions, from minor infractions to serious criminal acts. By examining deviant behavior, sociologists seek to unravel the underlying causes and consequences, ultimately shedding light on the mechanisms that shape our societies.

One of the key takeaways from this book is that deviance is not inherently negative or pathological. Societies establish norms to maintain order and cohesion, but these norms are not fixed or universally agreed upon. What is considered deviant in one society may be perfectly acceptable in another. Moreover, deviance can also serve positive functions, such as challenging existing norms and paving the way for social change.

Throughout our exploration, we have examined various theories that explain deviant behavior. From the classic strain theory of Robert Merton to the labeling theory proposed by Howard Becker, each perspective offers unique insights into the social processes that contribute to the development of deviant behavior. By understanding these theories, students can gain a more nuanced understanding of deviance and its social implications.

Furthermore, we have explored specific forms of deviance, including crime, substance abuse, mental illness, and sexual deviance. By examining these specific areas, we have highlighted the social, cultural, and psychological factors that influence the occurrence and persistence of deviant behaviors. This knowledge is crucial for students aspiring to work in fields such as law enforcement, social work, or policy-making.

In conclusion, the study of deviant behavior in sociology is essential for understanding the intricate dynamics of human societies. By examining the causes, consequences, and societal responses to deviance, students can develop a deeper understanding of the complexities of social life. Armed with this knowledge, they are better equipped to navigate the challenges of a rapidly changing world, contribute to social change, and work towards creating a more inclusive and just society.